Concrete Fantasy

Robbie Rodgers

DEDICATION

To all the dreams: affirmative and real, or simply forgotten
at the insignificant slivers of morning light.

To all my Mothers, throughout all my life.

To Friends, here and gone.

To Family resurrected and deceased.

To my Colleagues, working hard or hardly working.

To my Khan, my feline companion.

CONTENTS

"Tell them stories. They need the truth, you must tell them true stories, and everything will be well, just tell them stories"
–Phillip Pullman

"Gravity, release me
And don't ever hold me down.
Now my feet won't touch the ground"
–Chris Martin

"I was dreamin' when I wrote this
Forgive me if it goes astray"
–Prince

Concrete Fantasy Act 1

Walking down the hall,

in shoes made of rose pedals.

Wings fluttering at the ankles,

fly Icarus, fly Icarus, far away.

Cellphone ringing in pocket

pick it up, what do you hear?

Just some smoker's hack

and shattered glass, what a drag.

Passing by a woman in a red vest

with a melancholy feeling etched in dimples.

She holds all the power on tiny cheap plastic,

but questions every answer with monster

stained eyeballs.

The light at the end of the tunnel

shines bright threw the keyhole.

But the key does not work,

turns to sand, in my hands.

Black pepper flurries overhead,

ruffling the senses.

Old man comes to save the day.

Driving his lawn mower, cutting the asphalt.

Down deep in the jungle

a witch's cackle echoes in the treetops.

Scaring away young warriors,

if only they could shift the gear to drive.

The lady in the red vest is scolding me

for giving away all the treasure.

If I did not know any better

I think she will crucify me.

A fox skip's across porcelain tile.

Chasing down the Gent and George.

Hunting them with a silent grin.

Must be living the dream.

A woman with a German last name

inscribed on Denver Hickory.

I saw her, yeah, I saw her,

laughing away at the butcher's block.

A man in the chair goes wheeling by.

He has folk roots growing out the spindles.

I tried to reach out and touch them once.

All I got was a fist full of splinters.

At the end of the hall

a mirror says it all.

Soy un perdedor,

sprechen sie deutche.

Veering left to the window.

Look, here is the prophet Isaiah,

tending the garden, a promising place.

Ghosts go skipping through his pepper plants.

A reflection stare's back at me,

crooked teeth and canine's breath.

She is a specter in these parts,

wanting to go home, but her sentence

just begun.

I turn to approach her,

but she is gone again, naturally.

Off to haunt the professionals

    over in the cedar room.

Going down the stairs

Met with aged strawberry perfume.

The lady who made the rose shoes.

She smiles as she climbs, even though the

stairs are near infinite.

Reaching the ground, feeling a haze.

In the chase lounge, two poodle girls do lay.

Fog coming from their aura.

Maybe their lovers, I do not care.

Senses come clear as gravity ceases.

Floating on Styrofoam and optimism.

A Sister bumps the ceiling, cracking it away.

Never to break, some glass is just to righteous.

Out in the lean-to

a meerkat crafts his shine.

The smell, a real Cajun treat,

grounds me once more.

Fearing his hiss pushes me onward.

Bumping into the Italian decorator.

Smelling of fresh exotic gossip.

He spills more than paint out his mouth.

Shattered glass frees me from the latest

sproloquio.

Reaching the kitchen, clutter amok.

The lady in the red vest is hysterical.

The staff has left her, alone to fend.

I want to help, but wings are selfish creatures.

Gliding forward thru the window,

Opened by a Roman deity.

Her toga stained with **black** beast hair.

she laughs it off and pit-pockets my phone.

Outside and tripping over trash cans.

Filipino dust goes flying into the air.

Wings flutter though, knowing no resistance.

Except, the scream of a banshee in capris.

She is usually off doing her own thing.

Terrorizing the local commoners.

Today her cries echo, rattling the cage.

Thankfully, I am far away, surviving another day.

Off in the distance, two garden creatures scurry.

Behind the scenes they toil away.

A weasel playing grown up games, and

a badger, smelling of Irish whisky is close behind.

The town drunk and a harlot, are prancing in the streets.

Singing songs of French-Canadian beat.

Ignorant to the evening sun,

both reeking of cheap rum.

Houdini disguised as a captain,

orders a skipper to ready his craft.

A dinghy of red and black sets off.

Carrying false treasures, eyes set

for Neverland.

The smell of sand, the touch of lavender.

Waves descend with ease.

Foam fizzes vaporized by moon beams.

This is the sound of my soul.

A poor boy crafts shapes in the sand.

Though his stories are seldom told,

a laugh escapes his dirty face.

As the waves wash away his empire.

His mother calls him, back to the house.

She is my mother to, but not of natural causes.

Her eyes shift's focus to me,

although from a far, the effect is profound.

I should go home I suppose.

My shift is all but over.

Wings have become wrinkled in the wake.

My mind feels ready to sleep.

Grey rain is falling,

letting it fall into my skin.

Causing flesh to evaporate,

I do not make a single sound.

turning back, one final glance.

The house still stands

with lights full blaze.

Beckoning poor souls to increase their debt.

The woman in the red vest,

the specter in the window,

even the hounds on the lounge,

all keep carrying on.

Wet rain, now pouring all over me.

Soon, nothing remains,

white wings dissolve away.

Just imprints in sand,

nothing ever so grand.

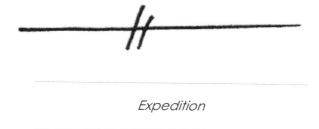

Expedition

Readying to embark is the biggest challenge.

Will nature cooperate or throw a fuss?

Best check your guide one final time.

For you will forget, later down the road.

Prepare if you must, take all that you need.

You may never know when you will come back.

Although it is true, you can always go home.

Do not get too comfortable in the routine.

Let dreams light your walk,

but do not follow every path.

Some trails lead to dead ends.

Detour through the grass, the ivy is just an itch.

Take a few companions to help past the time.

Someone to hold your hand, another to steal

your mind.

Do not escort to many, you will stress yourself out.

However, a furry friend or two never slowed anyone

down.

Beware of highway men along the shoulder.

No not for where they come,

they will still spontaneously appear.

Profiting from victims' treasures, they hold dear.

Indecision will try and rob you blind.

Anxiety will stab you in the neck.

Fear may sink your stomach

or give you a heart attack, fifty/fifty.

Improv will be your biggest ally.

Riding on its steed of confidence.

Towing behind is nervousness,

its best you introduce yourself early,

before awkward leaves begin to turn.

Prescribe your wisdom to souls in need.

But, do not be afraid to take your own medicine

from time to time.

the expedition is full of trials and tests.

Know when to stop and rest, even bones need

time to sleep.

The quest is never over.

Even if the journey has reached its final steps.

The edge of the map represents the familiar

ends.

But you may never reach the world's end.

Liza and the Rooster Barron

If your traveling High upon the Hills.

Where the trees, gold in the breeze.

Dance to the sounds of strings plucked away,

in the melody of some deep-rooted Americana.

Residing in a cottage.

Nestled in the woods.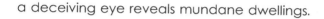

On the cusp of isolation,

a deceiving eye reveals mundane dwellings.

Journey on beholding the marvel.

A woman dressed in chalk,

parading down the walk,

with her companion gliding along the marble.

Feathers adorned her hair,

glistening grey in the shreds of morning sun.

Humming away while the gentleman strums the guitar.

A mesmerizing tune meant to draw fellow avian into
chorus.

Taste like sunshine and glows like honey.

Each step they take, arriving at a destination.

Outlooking over the Heavens Great Forest

within arm's reach of those holy stacks.

Outreaching wing embracing the embodiment of joy.

The Barron lays down all worries.

Exchanging Philosophical understandings,

For weeds dancing around his feathered hip.

Mysterious ways life seems to flow

Answers appear in the simplest of moments.

Yet, explained in such unclear distain.

Just let the mystery be.

Choosing instead to live life like the rooster.

Pecking away at grains bestowed.

Beak chipped, yet untarnished.

Echoing voices to the flocks in hope of reply.

If you dare make the pilgrimage,

upon the majestic hilltop.

Where leaves in the trees

share whispering words,

of feelings left undefined

Look upon this site,

of the Rooster Barren, black feathers royally adored,

and his lady flowered in grey.

Tending to their enchanted abode,

where chickens do fly.

Hot Chocolate Passion

Walking down the street,

a skip in my step.

My hearts about to leap

off the park bench, *splat,* onto the sidewalk.

I want to paint for you the moon and stars.

As watercolors do bleed,

swirls of gross affection add effect,

on a canvas misted in happy tears.

I think I am in love,

But it makes me nervous to say so.

No justifying cause presents itself.

Left only with a thought, is this false

happiness?

These feelings maneuver with a graceful

rhythm.

A dance of foreign invaders, swift, yet

elegant in design.

To look upon you only intensifies the beat.

Contact of skin on skin, electrifies movements.

You take my hand,

so soft,

so effortlessly.

Tiny cosmic explosions erupt at the

atomic level. A fusion of chemicals forms a balance

that transcends modern science.

Electrifying to the sensation, all I need is you.

Back in a familiar setting, on the couch of grey.

A scene that stinks of romantic comfort.

cozy wrapped in fleece and each other.

Your head slowly collapses on my shoulder,

numb from the impact.

This is what love is.

A simple Evening,

treasured by fools in cold

isolation. Envied by those

on fire with contact.

An undefinable emotion enters in the moment.

For a brief second nothing else matters.

Not this clichⵏ, not this poem.

Just you and me, together, synced to our own

rhythm.

Untitled

Love is the only thing left that is

real. Guided by compasses, but

our poles are off. Not centered, but

altered ever so slightly.

We find it real

hard to notice the misdirection, but

in the aftermath we feel the

effect. You can always use what is fake to

cover up the real. Instead of following our

hearts.

Like some childhood

fantasy. We instead find what works and use vivid

Imagery, to persuade our

hearts. Fooling ourselves,

believing we are making a

difference. Our bodies are

puzzles.

Lonely Yodel No. 1

Bow, ow ow, ow oh.

Bow, oh oh oh.

I am so lonely

Bow, ow ow, oh oh, ow.

My baby, she left me.

He he he he, ow oh.

Now I am.

now I am.

now I am.

Such a fool.

Bow, ow ow, ow oh, ow.

My baby she left me.

Bow ow ow oh.

Left me, so alone.

Bow ow ow, oh ow.

My baby, my baby, my baby.

Left me so cold.

Now I am leaving.

Do, do do bow ow.

This place in this bar.

Do, do do bow ow.

Where my tears,

disappear,

like dreams on a shooting star.

Do do do dom doo, doo.

So, I am ah walking.

Bow ow, ow, oh.

Walking away.

Bow ow ow, oh.

From this past,

Bow ow ow oh.

That haunts me,

like these strings,

on this old guitar.

Yodel-a-ee, yodel-a-ee.

Ah yo, yo, yo.

Yodel-a-ee, yodel-a-ee,

ah yo, yo, yo.

I am so lonely

Bow, ow, ow oh, ow.

My baby she left me.

He he he, oh he.

And now I am,

now I am,

now I am.

So through.

Bow ow, ow ow, oh ow.

Shall I Dance Alone?

I don't care if you stay or go.

I don't care if you say yes or no.

I don't care if you soar or dive.

I don't care at all.

I don't care if you cry in your dreams'

I don't care if you scream at the walls.

Hoard all your treasures only to burn them all.

I don't care at all.

Let the government fall

implementing more futile laws.

I don't care if religion stumbles.

I'll sit back and watch culture crumble.

I don't care at all.

I don't care if the waves go crash.

I don't care if your castles go smash.

I don't care if the sunshine hurts your eyes.

It's brighter there, no surprise.

I don't care at all.

I don't care if you sue for rights.

I don't care if you steal my art.

Your nothing more than a debutante.

I don't care if lightning strikes you twice.

I don't care at all.

I have Been a Fool

I have been a fool.

Chasing after you each time you strayed.

I should have been leaving.

Now, I have a long time to go.

I thought I loved you,

I thought I loved you so much.

Something just was not there.

Now I got to be going,

though the journey is vast.

You go off, up your way.

I will go down, down on mine.

This highway, barely a highway.

Faded stripes in the road never to cross.

Bells jingle at my ears,

from the jester's cap upon my head.

A sound that now echoes through my brain.

Hollow as a tree stump, dead.

Up in your place,

down in my place.

This old highway, not even a side street.

Just crumbles with each step,

from your enormous weighted step.

I once wore an outfit sprinkled in stardust.

then my allergies flared up and coughed it all off.

Now I see your face, whoa what an ugly one.

Nothing else makes much since except for

those last lines.

I have been a fool,

oh, I have been a fool.

Chasing after you each time you strayed.

I should have been leaving.

Now I have a long time to go.

<u>False Prophet</u>

I just do not care what it is you have to say.

Preaching from the top of your pedestal.

Constructed on the legs of hypocritical advice

and cheap pinewood.

Delivering a sermon that conveys a message.

Compartmentalize your doubts,

what good are they for?

What lessons are there to learn from your

failures?

Obviously, those you have yet to master.

Your disciples gather around your feet.

Hoping to absorb the golden ooze emitting

from your pores.

Prized treasures to those with minds,

malleable to your force.

Just another slime to wash clean, I suppose.

Although the substance looks shiny and pretty.

Magnifying the glow, you will find,

the cells of a being with too many self-loving proteins.

It has poisoned the nucleus to the point it no

longer knows its fatal flaws.

As an outsider observing this all,

I see the masses gathered at the mall.

They comfort and praise a would be

broken man.

He who hides his pleasures behind the faĺade of

tragic life.

He is a God to them, that is plain to see.

An omnipotent being who has given up on you and

me.

No longer his supporters, we turn away.

Isolated from those wannabes.

What I do not understand, can never be seen.

How a man with his life planned so beautifully,

throw it all away, again and again?

To prove some point. A dominance test.

So, build up your fence, but beware you will get
fried.

Not by those leaving but entering your pride.

A foe will approach your platform and
standing tall,

may finally clean your stain for us all.

Although you will twist some words,

call it a day.

Justify your actions, rearrange the blame.

Then go blow off some steam while your posse
stand's watch.

Defending your honor with their thoughtless posh.

Today this hyena does laugh at you.

For always calling him the fool.

Now, look in your bed, look to your side.

Lying next to you is the new master, surprise.

It is time, I pass you my hat.

It is now your turn to play jester, I am tired of

that.

A true fool thinks he is in control,

when the manipulating vixen stands watching

in your door.

You leave me with some wisdom,

some truth to share

Don't let your problems control you,

cut away that which hurts.

A thorn in my side no longer in place.

Plucked away, ooze no longer a sore.

A scar remains now in this wasteful space.

So long dear friend, enjoy false freedom

forever more.

Pretend

Going to a town.

Gonna stop trying to figure it out.

Might get in trouble, oh what the hell.

Go to parties, stay up until four.

Don't even care, just call in forevermore.

Got to live fast and die young.

Before old age pulls out its gun.

What is the point in trying to fit in?

Figure it out and get back to me please.

I do not understand the things that we do.

It is all imaginary, like the joy of sniffing glue.

Why bother punching in every day?

Wouldn't it just be better to just not stay.

Think I will go outside and cough up a lung.

If I am careful it will be the left one.

Could not imagine living without,

so, I purchase the goods in bulk.

Fooling myself with false joys are ok.

It beats trolling the internet thinking I am gay.

Might get high on something I just do not know.

Shoot up some chemicals found deep in my soul.

Stare at the stars while the high, coming down.

Brings me to a place I have already found.

Why do my feet levitate above the ground?

At twenty-three I started to figure it out.

By twenty-four, I am not so sure anymore.

Something so simple is not that hard,

but something so hard is not that simple.

At least a blessing, I do not have a pimple.

Let us pretend and play a silly game,

called how to walk semi straight.

Take your right foot and lead the way.

Left foot behind because why bother.

Marriage is impossible, I am no father.

This is it, a moment to forget.

Like all the rest, left dying under direst.

On the tombstone
please right:

"Die Alone" in the
secret chord.

The stray clowder can
visit up above.

I rest peacefully below,
hoarding all my love.

Highway

Gazing down a road,

asphalt sizzling as the

sun's rays blast the skillet.

Legs shaking in rhythm to the Kenwood's

blasting "Maybellene, why can't you be true?"

Storm clouds in the distance symbolize this journey

is about to get vicious,

or at the very least, slippery.

I'm not running from the past, I'm chasing

the future.

Drops hit the windshield "drip, drip."

Is this the best you can do?

An electric light show, prance along the

horizon. As Go himself has turned off the

burner and left the kitchen.

I am on my own now, as it's always been.

The terrain transforms from plains of green to

fields of gold. I wonder if this is what Sting was
preaching about,

all those years ago?

Throwing knock-off Ray-Bans in the floorboard,

letting my eyes readjust to the change.

It is in this moment realization slaps my face,

as the soft top remains down in the trunk.

Consider it my act of rebellion against Mother Nature

and all the Earthy deities. I simply do not care.

Their parental voices boom across the

darkened sky, scolding me for insubordinate behavior.

Laughter echoes from my car, like the hyena I am.

Dial turns up, as blankets of wet fall on me.

In this moment to hell with the future,

this is my destiny.

———————————//———————————

Whispering Air

What will be, will be.

Spoke the air in the quiet room.

Its presents, neither comforts nor burdens.

Blowing the possibilities away into a haze.

Anger is a fire, fueled with each shovel load.

Thrown into the blaze, ready to pop.

Invisible barrier stops its spread.

leaving it smoldering now, inside my head.

The breeze blows gentle on the stone.

Sealing the tomb from the soul.

A conversation left lay to rest.

It is probable for the best.

Tensions slowly begin to pass,

with every second the wind slowly stops.

Settling on the surface something familiar.

A tired old phrase ready to deliver.

What will be, will be.

Spoke the air in the quiet room.

Its presents, neither comforts nor burdens.

Annoying the senses into meaningless content.

What you Did Not Know

What you did not know,

about that day. I saw you in

the checkout lane register nine.

You taught me your craft, I

replied with my humor and eccentric charm.

What you did not know,

about that date. I was polished and shining.

Gel glued in my hair, made my feathers

glisten. On the outside, was confident and glowing.

On the inside, I was tremoring with worry.

What you did not know,

about that night. I didn't realize

you were someone who talked during

movies, a quality I would strain to

overlook.

In the car, we sat for hours,

swapping tales in exchange for

gossip of the day.

Like an unopened book, recently found.

you blew the dust off me, and opened me up

to listen to my stories, no one had heard before.

What you did not know,

afterwards, I raced my chariot back to

civilization and to my mates.

There my mouth ran with no end, sharing

with them the transpiring's of the evening.

A state of enthusiasm surrounded me, defending

me from all negative foes. Nothing

could have broken the seal.

Almost anything.

What you did not know,

the day you broke the seal.

With little resistance you sliced

a knife through my mailable shield.

That Night I did not cry, I just could not

emote.

Feelings of anger,

remorse,

sadness,

pain rushed my mind.

I could not get a firm grip on either. I just

sat in the silence.

What you did not know.

I am still haunted by the night.

not like a specter that looms over

me. More as a spirit who appears

only to tease me. Rehashing forgotten feelings.

Whenever I am on the verge of

reopening my book. The spirit stands atop,

sealing it shut. Leaving whoever approaches,

only half the tale, never a full story.

****

What you did not know,

time it seems, continues to blow more

leaves onto my path. Yet, they do

not seem to accumulate, carried

away into the breeze. A cool breeze

only provided by an age of self-discovery.

It calms the old spine and ease the tense

pages.

I hope you do know

what you did not before.

You are a fixture of compassion,

a source of strength for others.

Although our time together was short,

you transformed me for a moment.

Creating a person of peace.

I hope you may someday find the same peace.

I have faith you may know more than

I have ever known.

Dreams in Gothic

Traveling down the whispering road.

A path painted red.

Taking you to a place,

where sun never shines on Wednesdays.

Little black birds call out in the cold,

paying respects to the dead.

Fluttering about in an endless pace.

Finding some comfort in this idiotic craze.

Walking so slowly,

further and further from heaven.

Is there a heaven?

I would like to think so.

Shadows staring across the way.

Laughing, at the colors lost from my face.

They beckon me onward

down rabbit holes into the unknown.

Their lies a comfortable uncertainty.

If only we open our eyes

the answers would present themselves

in uncomfortable certainty.

A thousand steps down the road,

leaves no mileage left to show.

Just trivial experiences and worn down

sneakers.

Will Vienna still wait for me?

"Dreams are only dreams"

shouted someone out of nowhere.

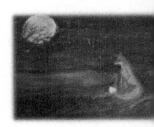

A chilling reminder

that everything is real.

To be Forgotten

Is it possible to touch the stars?

Just a little tap of their whimsical nocturnal

magic.

Enough to trickle down into my heart,

to give it enough to illuminate its path once

more.

I dreamt and woke to find I was an island.

That is why you kept passing me by.

Still I hear your words echo in the breeze.

"You won't get left behind."

Then your left behind, left behind to fight.

A struggle for survival in the great unknown.

Predators are swarming around, trapping you alone.

Just one slip and fangs uncertainly bite.

Stinging with hurt from a bloodless wound.

Nothing to alleviate the festering pain,

only to evaporate under a soundless rain.

Where the water does not wash away, just

refreshes the murky emotions.

This is the point where things start to

transform.

Here comes the nighttime.

Gazing into the sky, blinding by satellites

beaming down a message, eager to receive.

"The Earth is too big; someone has to go."

Commentators weigh in, delivering a sermon

of ignorance.

Darwinism at its finest.

Leaving one verdict to blame, the missing link.

Such an honor it must be

to be elected to leave.

No sense exercising the right to flee

just accept your fate, let it be.

Time will avenge your sorry state.

The world will forget you.

Left alone, gazing up at a checkered sky.

Wondering how magic can exist in a place of

exclusion.

Photograph Reflection

If you were here today,

what ancient wisdom would you say?

Would you embrace with a gentle squeeze?

or would you burn me down with your

cigarette sneeze?

Do I make you proud?

Watching me up from your cloud.

I felt your stare everywhere I would go.

judging a self-conscience left low.

False expectations are a drag.

I am sorry I never became a college grad.

Could I instead borrow some time?

Before the future slips away, slippery slime.

Wisdom bestowed on ignorant ears,

Still resides, though eroded over the years.

The words deaf in the mind,

Sing a chorus in the heart, so refined.

I did not get to know you well,

fate instead cursed us with its wicked spell.

Imagination left to shade in the scenery.

Still, an image I hold so dearly.

Missing you is a tired craze.

Wordless sentences make a better phrase.

This idea just likes to fester.

I am sorry, I did not mean to pester.

I eagerly await your reply.

Am I a failure in your eyes?

Do you still love Me?

Some days I do not know what that means.

Driving in Hard Rain

Falling

into the big empty.

crying out

"somebody save me".

Echoes in my head

tell me to stand tall.

These battles are yours to fight

alone. Cries fall silent again.

My life is like the river.

Flowing down places I do not want to go.

Memories float along the bank,

Suddenly, swept away by the rain.

Fantasy comes in a seven-letter word.

Escaping to a time

where childhood adventures still reside.

Not to be forsaken by dreams

gone by.

Falling

into the big empty, desolate empty.

May you forgive me,

of my sins I keep inside.

Find me somewhere, over there.

Gibberish

Take, my life from me,

my dreams do not really make since

anymore.

Just tangled up emotions, in a web of

uncertainty.

Waiting to be devoured by fangs of time's

mighty killer.

Take, my fortune and fame.

It has left me nothing more than alone and

afraid.

Isolated on a plain, only seen, never

adored.

My friends all think I am crazy anyways.

Take, my pleasures from me.

Only temporary relief for a pain not fully

healed.

Wounded by the arms of another,

in a battle to understand what war is really for.

Take, this poem and melody.

the words are all chaotically logical.

Placed strategically out of place.

Creating a tone that just doesn't make since

anymore.

There's a sparrow landing on my shoulder.

There's a dragon roaring closer.

That is not even the strangest thing.

This fever dream, will it ever end?

Curiosity Revisited

Curiosity can kill the cat.

    The cat has nine lives for a reason.

Reason better left unsaid.

    Said to be on God's creation.

Creation and imagination go hand in hand.

    Hand in hand we go walking.

Walking in euphoria.

    Euphoria created by organic phenomenon.

Phenomenon that echoes forbidden.

Forbidden only intensifies the sensation.

Sensation, where the beat goes on.

On and on we go.

Go past onlookers.

Onlookers reflect mixed reactions.

Reactions of utter disgust.

Utter disgust turns to happiness.

Happiness reflected in a warm smile.

Smile, resonating from your face, warms my soul.

Soul reassured of actions.

Actions that never truly animate.

Animate, the eyes of my face open.

Open to the world.

The world in which I reside, and you do not.

Do not feel sad for me, it is only mere curiosity.

Curiosity can kill the   cat.

Pope

Guided by cobblestone,

to a destination adorned with the old.

Ivory pillars reaching to the sky,

casting shade on those gazing upon the mystery.

Tucked away from mankind

in a canary cage plated with gold.

Left sheltered in dwellings, not shy from bold.

Resides you, oh creature of wildness nature.

Adorned in silks, of tastes refine.

Mesmerizing those with each flamboyant prance.

A trail of red feathers dance

at your feet.

Soon swept behind

with the velvet upbeat.

Stepping out onto your stage.

Your porcelain audience reflect to you.

A comfort never lost from glaring faces.

Immune to their obtuse stinging.

Must be grand, never needing a fake ID.

Surrounded by adoring papal fans.

They all kiss the ring in hopes of popularity.

A falsehood, but sweet nectar for their beaks.

Pharaoh's cotton sure sleeps soundly,

with a mind at ease tucked in it.

Waking in a dream state all too familiar.

Sleeping in a reality of boundless restraint.

All this looking strain's my neck.

Fuels the heart running on fantasy steam.

Desires of this self-reassurance flood the mind.

Dammed up by a tethered conscience.

Although there is straw for the donkeys,

and we can sleep soundly.

one thought can still not be put to bed.

left teasing insomnia to submission.

A tale of David and Goliath,

instead of to fight, embrace.

Arms out reached to accept,

but never received, intercepted maybe,

from the divine.

Listening to the voice you do so well.

Falling on deaf ears, down from great heights.

Someday my conclave will have chosen.

Smoke of white, only to turn black.

Single Philosophy

With open eyes

still blinded to the obvious.

Answers all seem to fry,

while the world burns, marvelous.

I do not know which ways right or left.

Which was is up or down,

or why is there so much weight on my chest.

Oh God, what is going on now?

If I found a girl,

I would not know what to do with it.

One with passionate curls?

I will trade it in before I quit.

Very is lazy, that is a fact,

but communication is not so simple.

Tongues ties send the conversation back

to the cave man days, grunts were so simple.

Could it be my destiny,

to die alone in a full family?

Surely not, could not be me.

I will find me a lady and die happily.

false prophets spoke some lying words.

Sacred to those who know no more.

"Just you wait, learn to watch birds"

build a nest on your heart's door.

Exploring the woods of tinder pines.

Thinking to myself "You're a fool boy"

Why don't you take the road that winds?

Right to the person, sparking a rhythm of joy.

Loveless

When I look at you

I feel a million little sweet things

erupt inside my mind.

Yet, the aftershock is just not strong enough

to be felt.

So, I walk away in chaos,

Of concrete floors and cardboard boxes.

It is a sticky mess of a place.

Where nothing just seems to get done.

I wake up every morning,

thoughts rush my head

while the blood slowly crept in.

The empty pillow to my left

goes unnoticed by objective orientated eyes.

Riding in a car,

to a destination all too familiar.

The radio carries a tune,

while the overcast blinds my view.

Protecting my lifeless partner at a sudden stop.

A silly reflex that goes taken for granted once

more.

Is it strange to not be in love?

Everybody knows my name,

the nature of these games puzzling to the

outsiders.

I just do not care to reply.

It is a waste of energy, waste of time.

Continue loveless, in this world full in

bloom.

Chasing Ghosts

I am always chasing ghosts,

through the haunted forests,

that surround a home.

A lonely house, where no one has lived.

In a field, where beginnings grow again.

Petting wheats, which play at my hip.

A breeze, so gentle, comforts the shoulders.

Blowing away the clouds,

a glow reveals all.

Dancing, just out of view, but in focus.

Specters of pale moon light dance along the

forest wake.

Their intricate rhythms, free yet familiar.

Call me away from my melancholy stroll.

Swirling among the wreckage of the forest

floor.

These phantoms guide me among the

decaying tree corpses.

The branches sparkle in the haunted

twilight.

With newfound light, they come to life.

Arriving at our destination,

a familiar atmosphere transcends onto us.

In this plaza in the woods, spirits ignite a

dance again.

This time possesses with foolish possibilities,

I join in.

The first decides right in front of me.

Smelling of fallen leaves, it leads me into the

circle. Only to drift away, ascending back into

the sky.

the second and third float on down.

Giggling with uncertain laughter, the first

one approaches. Puppy dog smiling.

The third says truly little, but sings the song

of its people, a song that has journeyed the seas.

They both exchange heart felt kisses, then

transcend into the moonbeams, shining on the
gathering.

Pleasant feelings linger in their wake.

Soon forgotten by distracting emotions.

Intensity rising, as dancing progresses.

The fourth and the fifth, lead the shadowy

pack.

All attention drawn into the circle, onto the

spirits.

Their supernatural powers clutching my

soul.

The fourth swoops in first, a surprisingly warm

aura emits from the glow.

Brushing smoothly with my hair,

something about this spirit is rare.

Dancing carefree beats, while singing a song

of confusion.

Playing fiddle strings with my focus.

The fifth, comes close, yet uncomfortably

far.

A color a shade of Lillie, its nudges on closer,

but something is not right.

Reflexes kick in and soon it to, darts out of the

circle.

Just not ready to accept mortal contact.

Overwhelming sensations flood the forest.

Trees taking in gasps of air,

in out

in out

stop.

The dancing ceases with triumphant silence.

A candle blown out whether by divine

intervention or cosmic phenomena.

Left standing with only my ribs and thoughts.

puffs of grey, conceal the moonbeams,

severing our ghostly connection.

A rush of blood to the head only tells me so

much.

Pausing in the moment, to ground my soul.

Moments pass, still nothing again.

Walking away from this enchanted nightmare.

To a field where the stalks have retired for the

evening.

Air so still, that breath serves as a knife

to slice thru.

In this solitary state, memories flood back.

Escapades through a haunted wood.

Memories soon fade to dreams, soon fade to

nothing.

As if everything happened and nothing at all,

simply chasing ghosts.

Never seeming to touch,

never feeling enough,

something anymore.

Inner Philosophy

Oppression of the tongue

is a true sin of the heart.

Nothing good can come of this false

imprisonment.

Just weathering of innocent words,

until nothing worth living remains.

Starvation of the unknown,

only leads to a malnourished conscience.

Left isolated, away from simple

understanding.

Leaving only fear to supply sustenance.

Resignation of concern,

takes us down a road traveled all too many

times.

Arriving at a destination littered with shiny

pieces of filth.

Nobody bothered to clean up, just blown in the

winds, reeking of self-loathing.

Failing of the optimism,

causes a total system shutdown.

Forcing a hard rest to resume operational

functions.

Megabytes of data lost in every switch flipped.

Marriage of fear,

a union of two passionate lovers,

anxiety and worry.

a holy matrimony shrouded in uncomfortable

content.

Vows spoken, only to be broken by silent sins.

Fatal flaws seen frequent in strangers' eyes

Eyes that turn out to be

reflectors.

Casting light on our vital doubts,

until all that shines is pain, bright as day.

To Climb a Tree: Revisited

Time away

is time to grow.

Just to be free,

only me.

Escaping to a place,

of limitless boundary.

floating in a space

of weightless possibility.

Tranquility finally achieved.

Speeds descend.

arriving in a state

less visited.

Embracing the vacuum.

Of endless imaginary bliss.

A Few Small Repairs

A few small repairs,

are sometimes all you need,

to get the past behind you.

Enough to drive away again.

Just tinkering away in the shop.

Tossing back sweat at the expense of creation.

Toiling away a peaceful afternoon.

Building a life from an old hobby.

Take five by the fan.

Cooling this sudden rush of excitement.

Not wanting to burn out like the sun.

Steady progress is progress non the less.

Better get back to work.

Never set still or your heart will stop.

If you're not careful it might get the better of you.

You can always be sure when your facing forward.

Stepping back in admiration,

of how something came out of nothing.

Spontaneous designs coming to fruition before your eyes.

Wipe clean your face, and be ready for the

next.

1

Seven Seas

Floating on top of the water.

Waves ascend and descend,

in, out, in perfect rhythm.

Gently shifting focus from near too far,

here to there.

While Diamonds sparkle across the checkered horizon.

A boat built of hollow hope

balances atop the aqua landscape.

Rocking, slowly with the waters weathered breathing.

Going in no particular direction, but making

good pace.

A crew of one, isolated from the rest of the world.

Man, the sail, tugging with ease against the breeze.

Dancing along the side are crying gulls.

They cry not of sadness, but of instinctual content.

With each solitary moment passed, a

reflective pause settles in.

Gazing upon the puffs of cotton sprouting on

the rich blue sky.

Grasping at any logical explanation of a

destination.

Settling for the peace of yet again exploring

the seven seas.

Sailing for other worlds, other islands.

Mason Jar

He was walking,

wearing a grin that broke every mold.

Inspiring all the birds aloft in flight,

to come down to earth once more.

Happiness is easy,

a song he has never once heard.

Not that it would matter.

His soul is young not dumb.

The sweat pours

from his face, in the heat of battle.

Commanding his troops on lines front and

back.

Fighting a noble fight under the golden glow.

Embodying the spirit,

of a ram, in his unyielding masculine strength.

Yet something still holds him back.

Like a little lamb all bundled in wool.

He's a queen.

Singing love songs, seeking somebody.

He just can't get no relief,

but he doesn't mind, the show must go on.

Getting high tonight,

on the pleasure's life bestows.

Found only in some secluded depth.

Where creatures gather for social reassurance.

Champion of games,

played on the grayscale field.

His only adversary is the ref wearing a black scarf.

Throwing penalty flags and every cup spilt.

You will find him,

nowadays sitting on an auburn porch.

Sipping away at some earthly nectar,

from his Mason Jar, which bears his name.

Finding peace of mind, once in a lifetime.

Taste of the Wild

Oh Brother, where did you go?

Down to the river that tangles with the unknown.

To the forest that echoes something familiar.

Up in the hillside, glistening with the heat of

yellow optimism.

On top of the mountain, dormant under the

canvas of a million white wonders.

Across the great plains, guided by souls of many,

found dancing on the black sky.

Wild horses stampede in a crowded unison.

The clouding dust obstructs the truth.

Nostrils flaring, with each bitter breath, *in, out.*

Never to be tame, chasing, always chasing

the setting sun.

I saw an ancient arrow go shooting across the skyline.

An archer only identified by Whispering winds.

Even this gossip monger would not divulge its secrets.

Opting to fade away into the night.

The sound of a howling wolf of twilight bound.

Cursed to isolation under the spell of a false god.

Cried me a tune that made me start to weep.

Where have you gone my sunshine friend?

Travelers roaming the open road.

Trading tales for some dormant comfort.

No buyers today for my home.

The price is too high, even for one night.

Away in some cobblestone palace.

Princess looks out her window view.

The scenery is something less than plain.

Feeling the endless guilt, she can complain.

Oh brother, where did you go?

Off on a crusade to the forbidden land.

On a cruise off the coast of an isolated island.

Or just walking away, trying to touch the sun.

May you get what you want this time.

Let the change in landscape swallow you whole.

Write your thoughts on the sand,

so, the waves can deliver them wherever you

may go.

Where we are Going, Where we Have Been

When it was now,

feels like so long ago.

The moments have passed us by.

Look, where we have been.

Ancient scribes recording each heartbeat.

While stone masons construct the monument.

blueprints provided by elders of the word,

not questioned by simple men with

simple needs.

Hurry away with sticky fingers,

before the dream fades into the twilight.

If you are not careful the silver tether holding

us together will snap.

Unfortunate few have lost a life in this

profession.

Fortunate one, tonight is not the night.

If I tie a noose around my subconscious

will the negotiators take me seriously?

Legitimizing my claim to the throne.

All for the opportunity to remember,

where we are going?

It does not make sense,

the usurper to an empire,

forgetting his own diabolical plan.

Yet, here is an unprecedented occurrence.

This was bound to happen from time to time.

It can still be said,

without further ado.

It really does not matter what's answered

in red.

A golden compass cannot tell lies.

Pointing in right directions, most of the time.

Where we are going is somewhere out there.

Where we have been is in here.

No greater detail shed.

Just embrace the balance created in the scene.

Ask me away while I reside on the throne, the

king of something.

To Stare out a Windshield

The wind blows upon green leaves

whom clinch to life with desperate stims.

The struggle to hold on is only half the battle.

It is finding what to do in the endless void of

time's atmosphere, which dominates the rest.

Controversy: The Ramblings of a 23-Year-old Liberal Living in his Parents Basement.

Left lying in your bed.

Scrolling through the glowing screen.

Varieties of soft, hardcore flood your head.

Leaving only an insufficient memory.

Instant gratification

beats,

social interactions.

Realizing,

romance is such a bore.

Stepping outside, stars catching fire.

Ozone is combustible,

so what?

Light up another one,

no regrets.

We got five years, then it's Mars.

Building walls with electric cars.

Lock her up, behind the bars.

It is a family business after all.

Take the children down the hall.

We're through being cool.

Melt all the snowflakes,

"Who needs them Hun?"

"Making it great again!" shouts the fool

scorching under an orange sun.

Taking shelter from the glow.

in our nests we're told to go.

Mom's spaghetti sure tastes good.

When all you can eat costs adulthood.

It is to political now to speak.

Turn to enlightened poetry,

while you tweet world war three.

I miss dancing in the streets.

Oh daddy,

the levels are getting harder and complicated.

Please save us from our artificial reality.

Jesus left strung out in the corner, faded.

Do not go to town dressed in scarves and tails.

Ancient wizards cast slander spells in the way.

Best keep the furs in the closet, destined to fail.

Their booming thunder echoes weakening clichés.

Me to, me three, me four me five.

Trolls and goblins attacking the chivalrous knight,

who is trying to keep the ancient texts alive.

Equal rights for all, fight a good fight.

Let's all pack our things and embark on the journey.

"*Haven't you Heard?*"

The roaring twenties have resurrected

once more.

New horizons smell of promises galore.

"*Onward we go!*"

To the dawn of yet another, controversy.

Disconnect

Why do we allow hate to trump all other noise?

Why do we allow our emotions to get the

better of us in the heat of battle?

Why do we not talk to those close to us

anymore?

Why do we cling to our independence like a precious
rattle?

Love use to be resolute.

An united feeling to feed all souls.

Now, it seems that is not true

anymore. We starve others to afford our rolls.

In dark corners lurks those who feed on

chaos's bloom.

Swarming every stock, leaving no trace of

green.

Only here to draw attention to the doom.

They all put out fires with gasoline.

Looting from the middleman does not seem the

answer.

Keeping with the status quo does not seem the

answer.

Just doing my job does not seem the

answer.

Protecting the force, to Hell with the corpse does not seem the

answer.

With riots in the street,

Protestors marching at your feet.

It does not feel neat.

To realize white is not the only meat.

The sun has decided to hide.

Gas giant clouds patrol the skies.

Leaving tears on faces of those too scared to

die.

The after taste in our mouths becomes soured from the

silent lies.

In the end.

The love we give

should be enough to drown out

the hate.

In this world gone madder

That's what should matter.

Portrait or Landscape?

Wings of butterflies,

sprinkle in color,

across the green pasture canvas.

With each flutter a cascade of

vivid blues pop into scene.

Pedals of lavender,

swept up in the breeze.

Dance along green guards,

blades extended out in full attention.

Stationary knights, protecting their purple

princesses.

Cobblestone roadway

sunken into the earth.

Tanning brightly in the sun.

Guide traffic filled emptiness

to destinations that no longer exist.

Branches in trees.

Adorned in leaves,

elegant in design.

Once framed resting spots for the wary.

Now forever homes for the fattening squirrels.

Clouds of white.

Near motionless to the eye.

Still float along the water filled sky.

Concrete Fantasy

Like Lillie pedals in an enchanted creek.

Blissfully kissing the surface so.

Forgotten over time

it would seem

you and me.

The locomotion of life does not rest,

even if our fires all died out.

Break Room

Expressing myself in a state of boredom.

Manifesting itself in needless swiping.

Scrolling through the false addictions,

nothing is exciting, more of the same.

Fidgeting is the weapon of the champion.

His legs and thumbs sync a choreographed

dance.

Hypnotic fixation on that which is present now.

On the cusp of breaking gaze, a thought

festers, but drowned out by an inaudible hum.

Attention is sensitive in this lackluster state.

shift focus to a door, swung open, *enters stage right.*

Actors brush in, riding off the high of the

performance.

Exchanging costumes, then off again, *exit left.*

Isolation resettles back into the atmosphere.

Slowly eroding away, from subconscious

emissions.

Every day is like Sunday, such an uninspiring

phrase.

Can there be no end to this mundane phase?

Gazing at the face of time, answers that.

in its hand spells, *confined freedom, five minutes.*

———————//———————

Patience's Funeral: Ode to Echo

I want it now,

I want to feel it now.

Not some false phrase.

"what will be, will be."

I want life to present itself,

instead of this reality stand in.

There must be more, more to give.

Trying to survive on just the here and now.

I would crawl to you,

if my point would come across.

Lost in translation, I fear.

Under layers of doubt, voices drown out.

I want it now,

the burning fire.

Insides are frozen, too cold to touch.

Needing to thaw out before it dies.

The desire to be something, one more time.

I would dress in feathers,

colors jealous of the sun.

If it meant questions would be asked.

Answers could be spoken instead of not

open.

"Nothing ever lasts forever."

Cries the words of an old soul.

Who ship has come and been.

It is time for my passage to depart as well.

All that will remain

is used up parchment.

Ready to dissolve in the rain,

from tears of dreams feared,

came and went.

Fox: Revisited

A Rustle echoes through the timber

forest. Discarded twigs *snap* upon

impact. firecrackers *pop pop.*

Marsupials on the sea floor scurry off,

to the low wake. Escaping the intercepting

orange glow.

Dirty paws *smack* the ground,

bushy mop sweeps from behind.

Mouth agape and tongue flailing about.

Over whelming momentum guiding

the ember entity forward.

Not even the silent forest giant,

now toppled and decaying in its seniority,

can slow life down. Confidence overflowing,

clouds his youthful brown eyes.

A thunderous leap at first glance, is achieved.

With each ascension, a new high settle's in.

In this state of euphoria, the bold little fox

fails to account for the sudden change in terrain.

Although visualizing a graceful landing,

Reality does not deliver.

Fore paws slip underneath,

the unstoppable momentum forces the hind forward.

Resulting in the same old makeshift tumble.

However, soon to recover, the damage has already

occurred

Sparrows, observing from above flutter off

to spread this latest gossip.

Vanity fading, the wounded critter

trots off, to lick clean these tired wounds,

physical and emotional.

At a flowing stream,

the fox takes a drink from the murky water. Reflecting

on the image staring back.

A slim face

with a slightly unproportioned muzzle,

dull burnt orange fur,

Burgundy hues streak thru.

One ear clipped,

another self-inflicted scar from

previous failed boasting attempts.

Desires of being the forest alpha still resonate,

but being the local jester suffices for now.

A train of thoughts soon derail as a posse

of orange bustle pass. Distorting the reflection.

Water splashed tickles the nose, coming too.

Past failures matter not as the

little fox runs to catch up with these

social critters.

Momentum begins to build once more.

Hello There: The Blithering Narrative of my Friend John.

The world spins out of control.

To the sounds of some discount ska.

Played over repeat,

because the rhythm sounds good.

It does not make sense,

so, I do not ask.

When pants smile at you,

better smile back.

Wise scholars discovered

cats are the engineers.

Architects of our great crucible.

Feline paws solve every flaw.

In the midsummer night,

sacred deer prance in the forest.

On the shore, a lighthouse light flashes

on to the sea, into dark places.

Age old tales speak of

a man's false appearance.

the jaw absolute perfection,

but no feeling left behind.

Stick to the books.

They will not kill you.

Leave it to computers

to become the bad guy.

Songs tell the only truth.

You should never argue with a crazy mind.

It does not get you no where

Don't you know by now?

I heard it from the wire.

The body of an American,

found in a garden,

Black–eyed Susan's overgrow.

A paragon soldier once said.

"I won't let fear compromise who I am"

I thanked him for his time.

I should go.

Pacing back in fourth.

While the bricks are crumbling.

Sure, sounds like fun,

cried the voice of, wait, what was I saying?

Losing the point yet again,

that is alright pass me again.

Swipe away one last time.

Sooner or later, I am going to win.

Playing Basketball in green shoes.

Scaling convertibles in hot sun.

Cooking omelets in the twilight.

Buzzing in again and again.

these are the answers

that will never be known.

That is ok, silence is gold.

Just keep guessing, it never hurts.

Ode to a friend. A

Twenty-four-line response

would not suffice.

It is pretty, pretty, pretty, good.

That's nice.

Special Message

Say a few words

for what has transpired.

Share some thoughts

on what is to happen.

Today is the day,

to give thanks and praise.

Like the clouds hovering above.

Today covers us up in content.

The smells of morning ham,

flood the nostrils,

struggling to come to life.

A swift kick is all they need.

Sounds of wildlife scurry overhead.

A bear, growling and grunting while

searching for his next meal.

A doe, near silent in this moment,

prances along.

Losing track of where to go.

It is time to make it unclear.

Just one more block

Then I can get up.

Said a few words

for what has transpired.

Shared some thoughts

on what is to happen.

Oh yeah, Happy Easter!

Blossom: Revisited

Wake me up,

I'm trapped in a dream.

Losing control,

I feel a tug on my

shoulder. frogs skip across a

pond with white pedals,

no

magenta, that float on the surface.

I turn and see what can

only describe as

indescribable.

I am me,

but

who am I?

A kaleidoscope of rainbow

shines on a shadow

casted from doubt.

Oh dear,

I think I've slept long enough.

I will come too, some

time.

Pedals continue to rain down.

Essential Fever Dream

"We live in a rainbow of chaos"- Paul Cezanne

Coming to in a strange land.

Everything is familiarly out of place.

Nothing makes perfect sense,

but then again did it ever?

Walking down the aisles

Red uniform tattered and torn.

Escaping the monsters in masks.

Spreading venom with each slanderous cough.

Their poison only sours the reward,

of hidden treasure buried deep in the rough.

Prying from the earth while sweat droplets fall.

Coming lose at costs body cannot imagine.

Royals with names I will never know.

Demand their lion share of the gold.

For the time they sacrificed waiting on us.

Patience died an unsympathetic way.

Silver linings do shine through.

The rose garden has bloomed once more.

Sweet aroma emitting

grounds the nerves, if only temporary.

Monsters like to trample through gardens.

Must keep the roses safe.

Sacrifice yourself, it is for a worthy cause.

Survive, and you may be awarded another star.

Surreal feelings flood into present time.

The warming sun nourishes the flowers.

Each a pure representation of the color spectrum.

The light also cast shadows, from the distancing masses.

X marks the spot does not apply,

to monsters who have discovered the cure.

Sucking the colors from the motionless flora.

Until all that remains is the browning husks of

what was life.

We live in a rainbow of chaos.

Colors clash with one another,

Playing games of utter importance.

Only green comes out victorious,

breaking records with each breath taken.

An essential fever dream.

Coming to,

but never to break.

Just waking in the heat of battle once more.

Monsters know nothing better.

Limitless Overtime

I have lost you.

Where have you gone?

Somewhere far away,

Or just underneath my nose?

I walked towards a purple blossom tree.

The summer sun setting on my shoulders.

Thought you would be there, resting in the shade.

Instead it was just a cast iron shadow,

counting the rust across its black corpse.

I drove away into the night

Hoping to hear you in this vacuum of radio volume.

What came from the speakers was not you.

Just the crying from the Angels of Harlem.

I fall into a dream, plagued by reality

This cannot be right; this cannot be real.

Longing for escapism from this place.

Why must you tease me so?

I wake up feeling refreshingly tired.

The sun sparks a drive to propel forward,

but without you, it is simply autopilot.

It is quite peculiar, is this the new norm?

I try to think back, back to the start.

When the words were fluid,

and the emotions just flowed into life.

When slowing down was not a crime and rest

was a necessity.

I try to capture what's lost,

but like catching mist with your bare hands,

all I am left with is lingering moisture on my palms.

Dried away with the swift air of

essential business.

———————— // ————————

Piss off Cake: Ode to Ram

They're to many problems for one to fix.

Everybody wants to claim their stake.

Nobody seems to know how to cover a blitz.

They all just seem to under pressure break.

You accepted the cards you were handed,

but folded before the game even began.

Now you sit on the sidelines stranded.

Watching the shit hit the fan.

Questioning problems before they even arise.

Making predictions that are doomed to fail.

Take your chances, if so tell lies.

Don't give out any ignorant truths you turn tail.

Your mammas can not save you now.

Welcome to the main stage.

When the lights shine bright, will you take your bow?

Do not hide behind the curtain, filing your pent-up rage.

They're to many people.

All thinking I am evil.

Burning holes in their church,

breaking down their steeple.

Open your eyes to the sunshine that reveals.

Beat of Blood

Did you forget?

Pushing in carts in the beating rain.

Plowing through, soaking with pain.

the bald man spitting his normal refrain.

While you just listen, no voice to complain.

Asking questions like they're going out of style.

Nervous, on making your own decisions once in

a while.

Panicking, seeing the masses start to pile.

Thinking every answer worsened your trial.

Standing up for the average guy.

Letting your conscience serve as your guide.

Not always falling back on some false pride.

We all know no one is better than you or I.

When giving to charity became so picky.

You grabbed hold of something real sticky.

If you're not careful things will get tricky.

Using your own discretion makes you giddy.

Hanging with the big dogs are we today?

You better play it cool or they will all go away.

Away to their homes, and there they will stay.

Leaving you to survive in a yard gone astray.

Remember the peers who got you this far.

Did you forget them already, like the hopes in a bar?

Buying their love with shiny gold stars,

does not make up for the time your afar.

They have moved on, there's a new kid in town.

So, step back and give him your bow.

Your no match for the hero wearing your crown.

Receiving praise, you grasped to profound.

You traded up for the sword of Damocles.

Thinking this new title would reward you some ease.

Now you have no time to sleep, to blink, to even sneeze.

The Gods now observe, searching for every misdeed.

You cannot turn your back on even one foe.

Ulterior motives eager to soe.

Beware of blades they stab in your toe.

If you slip up where, where will you go?

Did you forget the path you began,

that got you to this false promise land?

Back then it was so simple to develop a plan.

A dream to get out of the rut of always feeling less than.

Congratulations on improving your station.

Your one somebody called a new sensation.

Make us all proud representing our nation.

Just don't hide your spots you colorful dalmatian.

Remember those who got you in this place.

Remember it is a marathon and not a race.

Remember to show compassion to every face.

Remember to keep it simple, tread at your own pace.

Never forget where you came from.

In a sea full of storms, you're the captain not the bum.

The lighthouse will always shine, your welcome.

keep the fire alive, never go numb.

Animal Spirits

Lessons taught.

The Meerkat taught me to think fast and act faster.

Do what you can and move unto the next.

The rough collie taught me not to be troubled

by what others think.

You are not part of the heard anymore.

The stag taught me to follow the excitement,

jump in and help when you can.

Never freeze under pressure.

The badger taught me a strong work ethic

and a sense of humor go hand and hand, but

do not let anger weight you down.

The cat taught me that people are strange

sometimes, but who cares, you be you.

Do not be scared to jump into the middle of

action. Keep meowing until your heard.

The frog taught me to always plug holes.

Never leave a spot empty. Give it enough

attention before hopping on.

The fox taught me confidence comes to you

when you stop asking questions and

stand in your own.

Find cunning solutions to overcome your problems.

The carabao taught me to get out with the old

and bring in the new. Any additional weight will

only burden your load, leave it behind.

The piglet taught me that being selfish

gets you no sympathy.

Do not gorge on one plate.

keep your horizons open.

The owl taught me to always plan

ahead for the next season.

Sometimes his talons overextend, but

his wise advice is always welcome.

The possum taught me that its ok to be

scared sometimes, but with the right family

having your back, you have nothing to fear.

The Apennine wolf taught me that to be

a good leader you must have knowledge of

your pack. Know your strengths and

weakness before stepping up.

The old white-tailed deer taught me the secret

to survive is to know when to shift your weight around.

Above all else respect your fellow woodland creatures

and they will respect you back.

The koala bear taught me that its ok after a

long day of work to kick back and take a break.

Eat some leaves and have a good laugh.

The horse taught me that if you want

something done right, you must speak scarcely

and put in the demanding work.

The retriever taught me to keep chasing the solutions

to your problems. Keep your motor high

and your attention keen.

You will go far.

Wisdom earned.

Eden *(Haiku)*

A cool breeze on skin

Tiny eruptions emerge

As grass dances away.

Mother

Yellow Hibiscuses clash with the pinks,

in a garden decorated in feminine ascetics.

Color spectrum working overtime, in this

lively patch of beauty defined.

When I am silent and away.

Off exploring the other side of the world.

It is you who sill hears my call.

Ready, with a gentle reply, oh mother.

When tears come running down my face.

Over some overreacted mistake.

It is you who pauses to wipe them away.

A student trying to understand why, oh mother.

When I think back to you,

wrinkled skin and freshly permed curls.

Reminding me that intelligence is not measured

in lessons taught, but stories shared.

Though age takes away, you remain, oh mother.

When I stand beside you at our desk,

A serious vail lay on top of us.

Cut through, by good hearted

humor.

Though you are a sister of many,

you will always be one, oh mother.

When the cries of the mind

collide with the pressures of the heart.

It is your advice that reinstates order from

chaos.

Enlighten clarity, like the mentor that you are, oh
mother.

Five petals descend into the air.

Plucked from flowers uniquely described.

Each its own destination, own story inside.

Except for one quality predominantly

compared.

Love, oh mother.

Summary: Ode to Bob Dylan

Where have you been my brown eyed son?

Where have you been my precious little one?

I have been to ruins of civilizations time could not

save.

I have walked on sand that freezes every foot

print.

I have fallen through a bridge, forbidden to the good.

I have met captains of ships that will never sail.

I have tasted sweet truth at the cost of a dozen

cold lies.

A sun, shining bright, casts high shadows below.

What did you see my brown eyed son?

What did you see my precious little one?

I saw a man with half his face on fire.

I saw a labor struggle on a weightless load.

I saw a woman who painted a light soul.

I saw lightning dance across a cloudless sky.

I saw a flightless bird, sprout wings, then die.

I saw nothing familiar in a room full of

strangers.

Tiny clouds begin to appear, hazing the view from
above.

What did you hear my brown eyed son?

What did you hear my precious little one?

I heard cheers coming from the

silent majority.

I heard a dog bark at the hand that feeds him.

I heard gossip from the wrinkled old lips of the

oracle of Delphi.

I heard a poet who sings his song to a deaf audience.

I heard rock and roll from some cats from

Japan.

Cluster of grey starts to form, droplets begin

to fall, drip, drop.

Who did you meet my brown eyed son?

Who did you meet my precious little one?

I met a woman who unified an army, while her

own body sabotaged her.

I met a young man who buzzed in every

answer.

I met an old lady adorned with bright feathers

and shaded in turquoise eyes.

I met a man who was blinded by pride.

I met a man who was blinded by self-consciousness.

Showers subside, leaving behind a chilly dampness.

Intensified by the dying embers of the sunset.

What will you do now my brown eyed son?

What will you do now my precious little one?

I am going to seek shelter before I catch a cold.

I will retreat to a place of colors the deepest.

Where forests still mourn the loss of a friend.

Where hyenas are crying, and foxes are

laughing.

Where love still resides yet tangles with

hatred.

Acceptance tries to alleviate but confusion

binds it.

Where warmth is measured by the number of

fires.

Where something is still better than nothing,

where boredom kills time.

Here I will reflect on what has transpired.

Thinking backwards, forwards, and inside and out.

Spreading my gospel to the souls who will hear it.

Then drown in the ocean until I hit bottom.

A white moon arises, illuminating shadows

who play with our heads.

Their silly games, offer distraction

from the silence of the night.

Better Listener

Waking up from reality.

Eyes are fuzzy,

mind is a blur,

limbs do not work.

In fact, brain is doubtful.

Something does not feel right.

I cannot quite put my tongue on it,

speaking of tongue, why does mine feel so long?

Like pink taffy rolled up in tight packaging.

Opening mouth, the pressure relieves.

Ah, much better, "*uff, now that's a smell.*"

Speaking of smell, *"who's cutting grass?"*

Speaking of grass, *"why is my bed made of grass?"*

Speaking of bed, *"where is my room, am I outside?"*

Speaking of outside, *"where am I?"*

A man in a grey shirt walks along,

the grey sidewalk, swiping away on his black phone.

Having a pale visage and pale hands,

size only Andre would compare.

"What a strange creature."

Politely, I approach the giant.

"Excuse me sir, but, where are we?"

Head turns to gaze down at my figure,

met with pale eyes briefly, then the hand.

"Get away mutt!" and the slap across the nose.

Out of impulse from shock, my head goes down.

For the count 1...2...3... ok, I am back again.

"*Well how rude, wait, where did he go?*" No

time to process pain, instead the isolation of

being trapped with freedom in a foreign land.

Feeling in my muzzle resumes, as the quest for

answers carry on.

"*Wait, my muzzle?*"

Crossed eyed stare meets

black nose and white fur.

That's not right at all.

Sudden realization soon hits.

As feet are paws,

nails are claws, and

all hope for humanity is lost.

Tail from behind wags in rhythm

to the song of panic in my heart.

For what ever reason it would seem

I went to bed a man,

well, a male all the same, and

somehow woke a canine.

"Well, this is an inconvenience."

Sure, some have called me a gossip hound before.

Maybe this is a dream?

A simple pinch, then its freedom bound.

"Oh wait, that's right.

With nothing better to do,

off trotting through the field.

The touch of grass causes a warm sensation.

Will I ever feel the same?

Sun heats the blanket across my back.

Causing taffy to pop free once more.

Dragging low, and about to fall out

Relief must show itself somewhere.

Oasis presents itself, on strategic cue.

The body on an inland sea.

Calligraphy designed sign stands at the mouth.

Good thing I cannot read anymore.

Splash, into bliss I do find.

As steam rises from impact.

Joy cut short as fur and water do collide.

Clamping the ball and chain to seal my fate.

"Oh, I don't like this at all!"

Paddling paws propel me back to land.

With touchdown, the weight intensifies.

"I can't take this anymore!" I want to break

free.

With a violent shake, my shackles come

free.

Turning to droplets in the sky.

Standing alone. in the puddle of my creation.

A shiver trickles down my spine.

The sun mocks me, with its emission of heat

Only to cause, tiny goosebumps to emerge.

"Wait, can I get goosebumps?"

Desperately seeking out some warmth relief.

Paws sizzle with each step up the terrain.

"That's it!" A thought summons itself in the canine cortex.

With a thunderous drop, I fall to my side.

Rolling away in these tiny stems of grey.

Absorbing all their heat, a selfish sponge I am.

Suddenly, euphoria achieved.

The sacred spot.

Pressure point explodes with every shake,

minuscule tremors of joy soon erupt.

In this moment of bliss, a noise so faint, shout's

out to me.

Breaking me off this expression of content.

"Sigh" I better go check this out.

Good thing curiosity killed the cat and not

the dog.

Trotting from the hillside,

paws deep in daisies I stomp.

Walking at a pace, surprisingly comfortable.

Damp fur dries by the breeze.

Off in the distance,

a woman's cries echo in the summer void.

Laying in the taller grass,

in an angle of utter depression.

I call out to her,

"Excuse me miss, are you ok?"

"Excuse me miss; can you hear me?"

"Hello ma'am, are you alright?"

"Arf, arf, arf, arf."

"Arf, arf arf, arf."

"Woof, woof, arf arf."

"Arf, woof, arf, arf."

"Man, she must be hard of hearing."

"Oh wait, of course she can't hear me,

she must be deaf!"

Must go with a more paws on approach.

Galloping at high speed,

taffy flopping on my side.

One thought race's in front,

must confront this strange deaf lady.

Approaching the wonder with cautious ease.

The cries of this creature flood all sound.

Head goes down, in tactical stance.

Observing all with 20/20 olfactories.

Wearing pale blue overalls,

colors popping with her dark complexion.

Discarded sandals lay by her hip.

A blurry parchment crumpled in her hand.

Progressing out of sheer instinct and

mild curiosity. Inching ever so closer,

until a *snap!* Goes the grass.

as if on cue, the cries stop,

intensity rises.

The lady turns her head.

Events unfold in my mind.

As if time itself was moving in slow motion,

and I in light speed.

With swift clumsiness, I prance back only

to stumble on lose fur.

A chuckle escapes her mouth.

If only I could blush, I would be a rose.

Frozen in this state of embarrassment.

Our eyes do meet, seconds turning to hours in the
glass.

Finally, the last trickle of sand does fall.

Ending our stare off, snap back to reality.

she turns away, as misty tears trickle down

her cheek.

If sadness were a smell, it would be her perfume.

Something had to happen.

With threat levels resolved to minimal.

I do approach, tail tucked for balance

and out of fear for the unknown.

"What is it collie boy? Did my cries disrupt your dog day?"

Came the voice of the angel, crackled and divine.

" You should run off and be free, run away

from this mess that's me."

Runaway I did not.

Continuing to her lap,

I smell her face.

It is not perfume of sadness,

it is fragrance of grief.

Out of reflex, taffy plops out.

Lapping up the saltwater remnants from her cheek.

A smile soon chisels along her face.

As a hand comes up, pushing me away.

"Buh, thanks for the cleaning collie boy."

Although a bit saddened by the unappreciated

response to my helping gesture.

The sound of that name triggered an automatic
response.

Tail increases tempo.

For a moment, a bubble formed around us.

Time itself could not penetrate.

As eyes met, as on cue, taffy drops out once more.

A laugh escapes, *"you know, you're a strange*

looking mutt, collie boy."

Again, at the sound of that name.

Tiny receptors deep in this simple canine brain,

fire off a response, a reflex.

Muscles turn to mush, falling forward into her lap.

Resting on top of her leg.

A gentle hand ascends on my head.

With a graceful landing, it soon moves on

at a steady pace, a relaxing speed.

These moments mean so much,

but feel so little.

Happiness equivalent to the numbness in

my neck.

Muscles power off, with each stroke.

"Go to sleep little collie boy."

A whisper in the breeze touches my ear.

"We can stay here a while longer."

The grass, warm on my furry belly is the last

feeling I recall.

In peace you find

A state of imaginable high.

Coming to in a state of black.

then it turns to grey.

Cold to touch,

metal to taste.

A man in a white coat walks in.

Beard of Abraham, staff of Moses.

He has all the answers or

just the ones they question.

Species re-transplant has completed.

Results are unsatisfactory astounding.

The experience has proven unequivocally,

that emotions transcend barriers undefined.

An inaudible growl escapes my mouth.

A foreign hand warmly strokes my fur.

"Oh, quiet you, your test is all but done."

Booms a voice, sarcastic yet final.

Echo silencing my soul,

forcing my full attention.

Hand retracts to its operator's side.

Eyes then reflect on to mine.

"My dear boy, I'm sorry for the confusion.

Your experience was merely an illusion.

A test of adaptability,

wielding results on companionship compatibility."

Among this auditory exposition,

one solitary thought echoed inside.

Puzzling my brain, trapped in a canine's.

"Why is this man rhyming?"

"Oh, apologies once more.

I thought your species communicated in this manner.

Certainly, your prayers to me can be a bit

singsong.

I have too many species to keep track of as is."

Firecrackers began to pop,

as more and more questions boomed into

my head's empty space.

Ignited by this never-ending scene.

Thoughts going boom, boom, boom.

"Non the less, are time together in this

fashion has drawn to a close.

Thank you so much for your

voluntold support,

may you find peace and joy in your life

and love all who, blah, blah, blah you know the

spiel.

Now close your eyes, it is time to take you home."

"And remember this, to be a better listener,

no exchange of words needed, just simply, listen.

"Wait, what do you me—————————"

and with that, nothing.

—————————

Waking up from a dream.

Eyes are fuzzy,

mind is a blur.

Thoughts try to grasp onto fading memories

of some far-off episode, but

alarm clock buzzing,

causes grips to slip, losing all that was there.

Gears slowly reignite motion.

As speeds resume normal levels.

Yet, something halts production, a simple intrusion.

"Why does my blanket smell like wet dog?"

Concrete Fantasy 2

Had it been.

One month?

One decade?

One year?

One day?

Who could say?

Wings resurrected

like Christ on his stick.

Flamboyant flare added for this affair.

Roses replaced with a silver reflection.

Change felt in the air.

A house has become a home.

Home full of nowhere-ness,

come on inside.

Stepping out of my room.

Wings *shiver* in anticipation

of what wonders lay afoot.

Let's take the ride.

Walking down the hall.

Passing **scary monsters** wearing masks.

Hiding fangs that drip with venom.

I smile towards their faces and flutter by.

The **stomping** from their callused plantares,

rattles the floor, sending wings soaring.

Over the galvanized railing,

into the land of the living.

The lady in the red vest catches my fall.

She snickers as she lets me go.

No longer under her thumb, although equals

freedom is not that easy.

Stepping outside to bathe in sunlight.

A familiar fox and badger scurry on by.

playing silly games, while the gardens grow.

I smile and take shelter under the cedar tree.

Mr. GQ trades his fashionable advice,

with the hunter and his pro bounty.

I try to get into that market, but

the magic man pulls my leash.

Houdini holding all the magic,

casts his whimsical spells on wings, turning

around.

The skipper marooned on an island of tall grass.

Leaving me on the new apprentice mantel.

A silver lining shines through.

Spells seem to fade away,

like all good things in the end.

I find freedom away from this traveling show.

Back on the scene, in familiar beat.

Passing back inside, into the kitchen this time.

Things are still a-mock, what a surprise.

That is what happens when the deity says

goodbye.

The starving guests line up in squares

six feet apart and mouths a gap.

I flutter low as if not to disturb.

If I am careful, it is like I was never even there.

The entrance chase lounge is empty today.

All the dogs have run away.

All but one poodle, but I cannot say

If she is real or not?

Is it strange to miss someone?

When that someone was never there?

just a thought that still festers in unknown.

Like an imaginary friend you just cannot

outgrow.

Thoughts cut short by a banshee's wild **scream**.

Who in the world let her in?

Although her disguise is uncanny.

The helpless still hark to her cries of false

direction.

Wheeling away from it all,

the king of philosophy.

I try to stop him, to pose

questions of troubling youth.

He just smiles and tosses me a

plump brown egg.

Saying the "real war is with reality."

He is gone again.

Greeted now by a familiar specter.

This time in human form, but still smelling

of canine's breath.

She looks to me to fix her toys.

Stomped to pieces by monster sized toes.

I smile and play along with her games

once more.

She grows bored of this old scene.

She vanishes into the chaos.

Only to reappear in the garden,

tending to flowers, tending to her soul.

Distracted by the window's view,

the nun bumps my shoulder, not hard

it is true.

We exchange a familiar laugh.

Spreading the good word, like missionaries of the

same church.

Our time is cut short, the all mighty calls her

to the front.

Although she would rather play the part of Eve.

She still comes out to face the noise.

Even if the glass shatters, she does not care

anymore.

I leave her to it and glide away.

To the back yard, only to find

a crabby harlot nursing bitter flavor.

While monsters **gawk** in utter confusion.

The meerkat shack is empty once more.

He is gone out to find something more.

Although his stock is full of supply.

He scurries on, leaving a note,

"get in line."

Wings soar on, only to collide with a man

dressed in black.

An artist, paining stories in every scar.

With potential to create a masterpiece of

unimaginable aesthetics.

Held back by forces in reach of another's

magical control.

Listening very still, for a **cackle** in the trees.

Nothing echoes back, just bonsai leaves hitting

the breeze.

Guess the witch is out of brew,

or the mighty warriors finally did her in.

The sound of a wise old owl distracts senses.

Usually sticking his beak into many holes.

Today he seeks refuge above the forest floor.

Observing all while his hatchlings do all the

dirty work.

Nowhere else to go,

but out to shore.

Only to find it close

down. Is there anything else to do?

The boy from the beach

starts following me.

He is an annoying sport,

but I never mind his company.

Telling jokes to pass the time.

We make our way down the sidewalk.

Kicking over trashcans for the hell of it.

Until a graceful butterfly flutters into view.

Distracting one curious youth.

He chases after it, onto wet sand.

Leaving me to wander into this seaside town.

That is all but closed down.

People just do not leave their homes anymore.

A laughing Labrador goes chasing

after the friendly Burmese cat.

In good nature and fun company.

The Arkansas mad man watches from his

front porch.

A StreetSide wrestler tries to survive

in a world gone mad.

Displaying his strength,

while venting his steam.

Delivering a devastating finisher

to an audience of dust.

A drifter wearing tattoos from

faraway places approached me.

Rambling in big words I could not understand.

I smiled and humored him for a bit.

I think he was making fun of me, but a fool he

may be, for wings know no insults.

What to do now, with so much time?

Throw frisbees at the sun?

Grab a beer from the shack?

The words from an Italian soliloquy gives me

direction.

Back at the house,

the Italian designer is letting it all out.

Trying to keep order in this organized fiasco.

"With all due respect" cries a rebellious voice.

Silenced by the leone tra le pecore.

A friendly ghost startles me with his words.

The endless monologue only bores me more.

Wings are not better listeners either.

Fluttering away from this haunted one's

refrain.

I feel sorry for his next victim,

a little boy trying to help monsters stay in line.

An ironic flip, a child with no fear in eyes.

Chatting with the ghost, with patience of a

senior.

A familiar friend approaches wearing

costume jewelry and a plastic crown.

Awarded for being the new hero of the land.

Wings are hesitant on accepting this new

champion in red.

But under the robes is a companion of the

long and winding road.

We exchange shared experiences before

another **monster** bashing summons him away.

Not my mother mother, stands in the back.

Shaking her head in disbelief.

Back in her day, the silent minority had

control,

Now the **monstrous** majority have run **amok.**

I go to hug her, more for my sake then hers.

Wings need a momma bird in all this mess.

Although not sure of herself, she embraces

with confidence. Giving me hope for our tiny

little nest.

Among all the shouting, I heard a dinosaur

was spotted roaming in the pool room.

Wrapped in chains and nylon rope.

After further investigation, it was just an

old maid, spitting her normal complaints.

A second citing recorded, this time in the

laundry room.

Drawing no attention from the hoard

demanding attention.

Curiosity never kills the wings, pushing on

the door, revealing another false claim.

Simply, a stray piglet seeking some assistance.

Locked in a foreign room, at freedom first's chance,

it runs away, leaving a mess to clean behind.

Good thing the prophet Isaiah is still around.

Blessing every mess sure is a busy business.

The lady who fashions shoes with wings,

smelling of dried sweat and baby's breath,

smiles toward me but does not make a sound.

Wings smile back in confusion,

is the maker not proud of us?

She turns away, back to her chores.

Leaving us alone in this house full of

outdated new.

Wings flutter with no direction on what to do.

Corner

                              to

                                                  corner

we go soaring.

There must be more than this?

Lacking substances in the mundane.

Adjusting to the new norm one day at a time.

Will we ever get back there again?

Brought out of focus one more time.

Grounded back on the cement floor.

Anticipation returns in unique form,

as wings flutter on, chasing the next

right moment to come.

To be Soaring

The birds take off from the branches.

Ascending to new heights, mere mortals

only dreamt about.

With little hearts fluttering, a dare is set.

To find Neverland, before the end of this

morning light.

End

ABOUT THE AUTHOR

ROBBIE RODGERS

Robbie Rodgers is not one of the most acclaimed writers working today. He is best known for being a scatter brain human being. Currently residing in some small town in Missouri, with his only child, a plumpish black cat named Khan. The author of two poetry books, Everything Gone Green & Concrete Fantasy, both are passion projects intended to entertain or bore all masses, one of the two.

Made in the USA
Monee, IL
17 September 2020